Colin Matthews

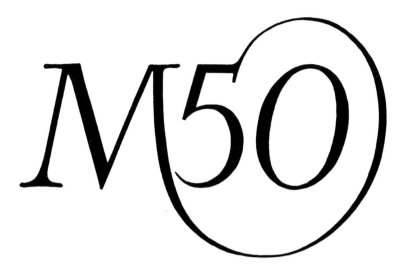

for orchestra

(1995)

FABER *ff* MUSIC

© 1995 by Faber Music Ltd
First published in 1995 by Faber Music Ltd
3 Queen Square London WC1N 3AU
Music processed by Olivia Kilmartin
Cover design by S & M Tucker
Printed in England by Hobbs the Printers, Southampton
All rights reserved

ISBN 0 571 51601 7

Orchestral parts are available on hire from the publishers

M50 was written for Michael Tilson Thomas's 50th birthday.
The first performance was given by the London Symphony Orchestra
conducted by Daniele Gatti in the Barbican Hall, London
on 19 March 1995

Duration: c.4 minutes

ORCHESTRA

Piccolo
2 Flutes
2 Oboes
English Horn
2 Clarinets in B♭
Bass Clarinet
2 Bassoons
Contrabassoon

4 Horns in F
3 Trumpets in C
3 Trombones
Tuba

Timpani
Percussion (2 or 3 players):
    1. 4 Tom-toms, Bass drum, Vibraslap, Metal ratchet
    2. Suspended cymbal, Sizzle cymbal, Hi-hat, Tam-tam, Guiro, Glockenspiel

Harp

Strings

Score in C

for Michael Tilson Thomas

M50

COLIN MATTHEWS

*trombones 1 & 3: if insufficient time here, remove mutes before bar 51

20

* all players independent